HOSTAS: MEMORIES OF A HOSTA LOVER

ELIN ENDSLEY JOHNSON

.

HOSTAS: MEMORIES OF A HOSTA LOVER

ELIN ENDSLEY JOHNSON

ISBN
978-1-954509-09-2

Published by Vision Run Publishing
www.VisionRun.com

Photography: Elin Johnson

Printed in the United States

CONTENTS

Elin Johnson

HOSTAS

"GATHER FRIENDS LIKE FLOWERS"

There used to be a place called The Fruit Market in my hometown of Sweetwater, Tennessee. They sold veggies and fruits in season, and in spring they sold plants. I looked forward to their spring offerings and bought both annuals and perennials there. One spring (maybe in the late 1970's) they offered two cardboard boxes full of bare root hostas for sale. They were labeled "Green" and "Variegated," and I bought one of each. This was my introduction to hostas. I loved both of them!

Then at some point someone gave me an issue of *Horticulture* magazine. This was the beginning of my love of flower magazines. But this first issue also initiated my devotion to hostas. There was an article about a man in Manhattan who had a lovely, shady garden between tall buildings, and hostas were featured prominently.

Prior to that, I had no idea there were so many different varieties (big and small--green, blue, and gold) and displaying many types of variegation. The photographs showed them with various companions, ferns, shrubs, and wildflowers. Not only that, a nursery offering many of them was advertised, and I immediately ordered their catalog. I was permanently hooked!

That was the beginning of an important part of my life. In 1998 I retired and started gardening in earnest. I joined the Friends of the University of Tennessee Gardens and became a volunteer there; and shortly thereafter, when the East Tennessee Hosta Society was formed, I joined it too. Its motto was *"Gather Friends Like Flowers"* and that's what I've been doing ever since. Hostas became the major plant in my gardens, and the club's newsletter became my job for the next 20 years.

I also joined the American Hosta Society. Their publication, the *Hosta Journal,* is worth the dues, in my opinion. It shows pictures of up-to-date varieties and has articles that tell you about any developments in the hosta world. By the way, there are thousands of named varieties, big, medium, small and mini sizes with many colors and different types of leaves. (Check out www.hostalibrary.org).

The AHS has annual conferences. (I've only attended the one that was held in Nashville.) But there are regional divisions that hold their own conferences, and I have attended several of the ones held by the Dixie Region. These conferences are absolutely wonderful. Not only do you learn a lot, but you "gather" new friends. The East Tennessee Hosta Society was scheduled to hold the Dixie Region Conference in 2020, but it had to be canceled. Then we tried 2021, but it was canceled, too. Maybe 2022? I decided to write this account to have at that conference.

This is not intended to be a manual on growing hostas, but is the history and the memories of the gardens of an old, dedicated hosta lover. You might say it's a love story. I thought it might be something of an incentive to newcomers. Create your own hosta garden. "Beauty is in the eye of the beholder." The possibilities are endless!

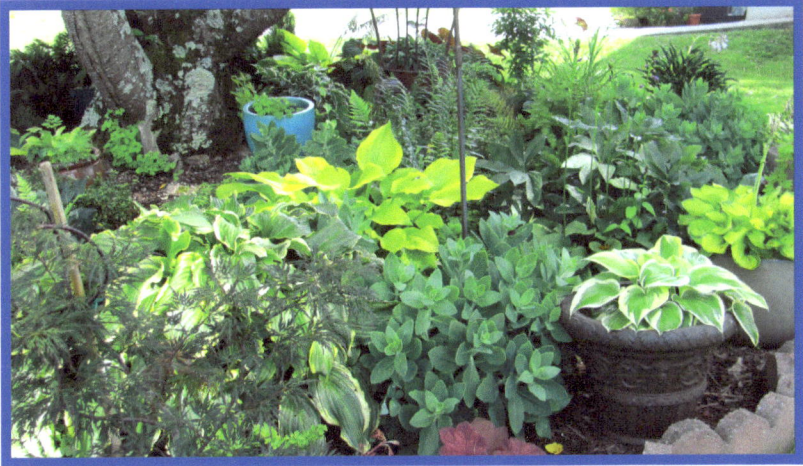

OBSESSION

The hosta vendor elaborated
a stunning proclamation.
A distinctive new development—
with unique variegation.

Then the familiar quandary—
new cultivar flirtation.
Exorbitant expense,
but irresistible temptation.

And so that great new hosta
gained emancipation.
Went straight home with me
to "perfect" habitation.

New acquisitions represent
sweet dreams and great elation.
This new hosta will, of course,
exceed anticipation!

— Elin, an addicted hostaholic

MEMORIES OF A HOSTA AFICIONADO

I'd like to show you pictures of the gardens where my hostas lived. My gardens have not been the ones you are used to seeing at the homes of many hosta lovers where many hostas are lined up in rows. I had a great many hostas, but I also had a lot of other plants to accompany them. My first garden had rooms on the different levels of a steep hillside. The picture above is the "lower garden" at my home on Chestnut Street in Sweetwater, the one I call my "first" garden. Many hostas were in residence there, and ferns accompanied them.

Below is a scene from the "upper" garden there. The shady back side of this garden bed featured both hostas in the ground and some in containers. The front of the bed contained lilies, garden phlox, and other tall plants and shrubs that shaded the back of the bed.

And then there was my home on Fairlane Drive. The property was flat and sunny, and the front yard had too much sun for hostas. So, the hosta beds were placed in the back yard. Here was a view looking toward the house.

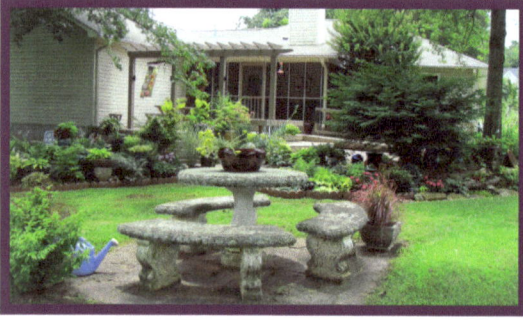

On the other side of the back yard was the "cherry bed."

And this was the bed at the end of the back porch.

Everyone who has room in their yard wants the big ones. One large variety that has been popular for many years is Hosta 'Sagae.' My 'Sagae' resided under a Japanese maple at my first garden in Sweetwater. Today's most popular large variety is 'Empress Wu,' a huge hosta; and its sports are being put on the market every year. One, 'Winter Snow,' is a variegated one I have seen and greatly admired in several display gardens.

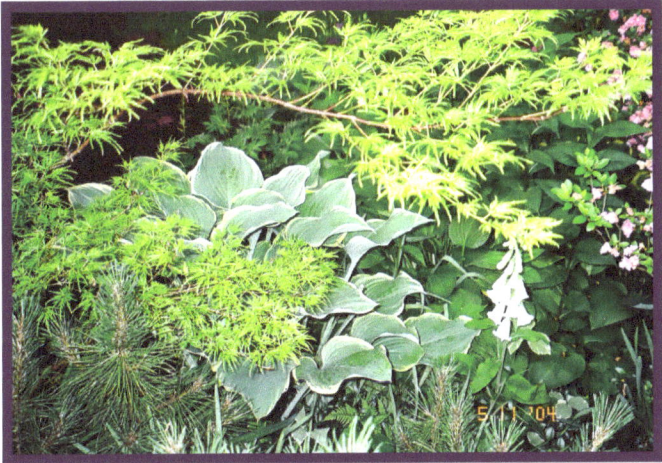

Hosta 'Sagae'

But my favorite big hosta of all time in my own gardens was 'Earth Angel,' and it also makes the popularity lists every year.

Hosta 'Earth Angel'

Some of my favorite big ones were not well known—a yellow one, 'Dandy Lion' and a big blue one, 'Thunder Boomer' were purchased at Dixie Region Hosta Conferences, where vendors always have many different varieties to choose from. Another big beauty that I really enjoyed was Hosta 'Spartacus.' It grew under the north side of the "cherry bed" where the trunk was covered with lichens.

'Thunder Boomer'

'Dandy Lion'

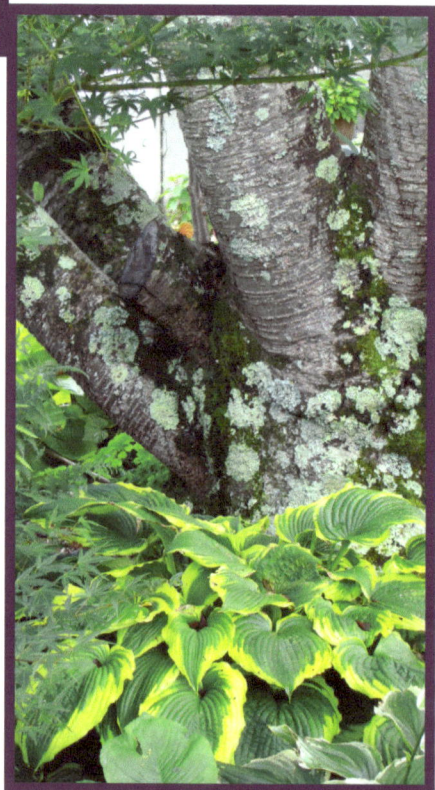

'Spartacus'

Medium to small hostas have been the most numerous of the hostas I have grown. I used to have more than 100 different varieties of hostas. Here are some more of my favorites.

One of the most popular varieties that is always one of the top five hostas on the popularity list is Hosta 'June,' a medium-sized variegated variety, gold with a blue edge. It deserves its reputation.

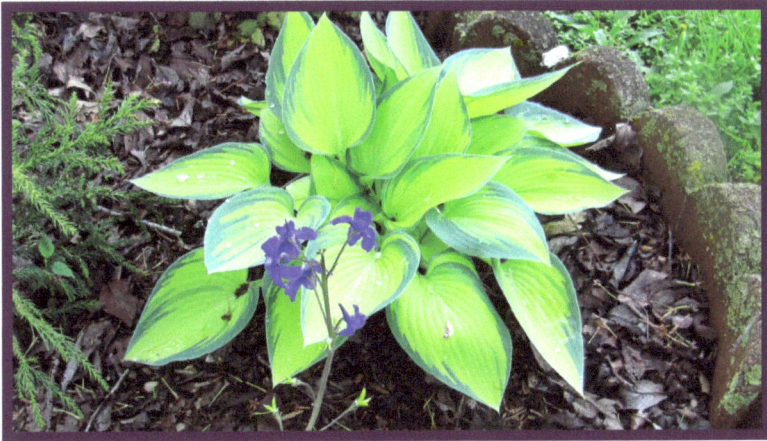

Another middle-sized beauty that has been very popular is Hosta 'Fragrant Bouquet.' And another one that I've really enjoyed is 'El Nino' shown here with 'Lakeside Neat Petite' and a Ghost fern. These two have white-edged variegation.

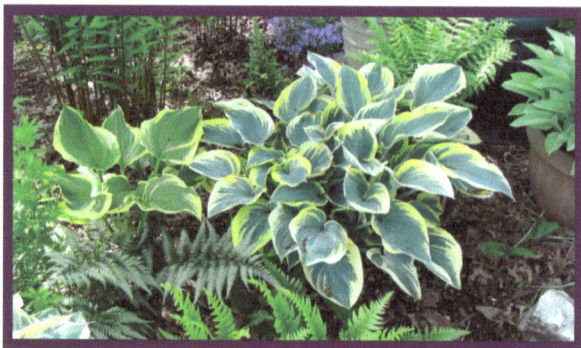

Left, ventricosa Aureomarginata; right, 'First Frost'

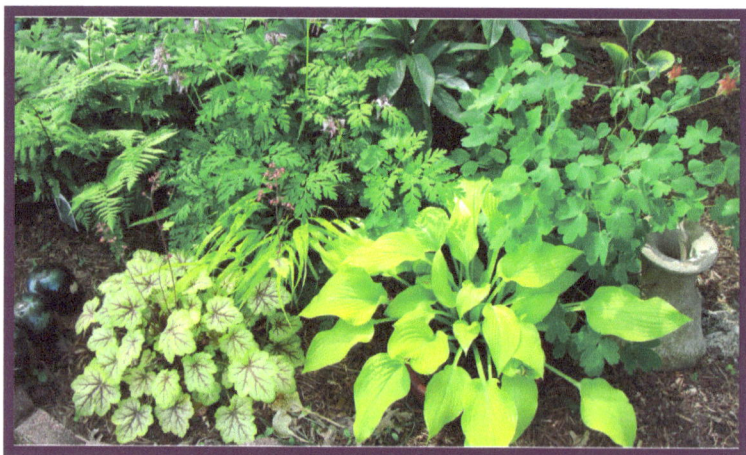

"Yarden Yellow Snow" with Heucherella 'Solar Eclipse'

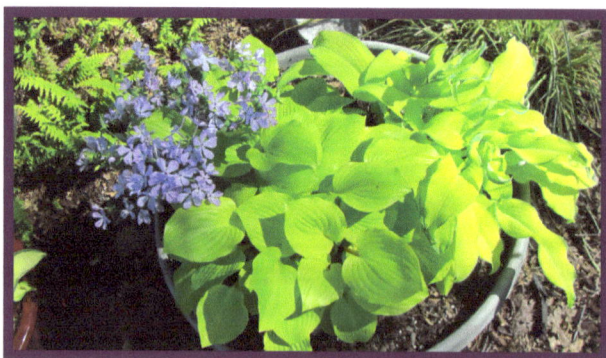

'Mango Salsa' and 'Ripple Effect' with blue phlox

You'll notice that many of my hostas are in containers. I find it easier to take care of my hostas, especially the small ones, when they are not in the ground where it's too easy for the snails and slugs to get to them. When these pests do show up, I use the iron phosphate snail bait, Sluggo, or one of the other brands that have been developed. The big box stores have their own brands of iron phosphate slug bait now.

'Dark Star'

Growing in pots turned out to be a really good idea, because I now live in a condo, and it was easy to move the pots to my new location. There isn't room for large hostas now, but I still have some 30 medium, small and mini varieties. Most are located along the back wall of my condo where the sun doesn't reach them until late afternoon. They seem to be happy there.

Top, 'Bachelor Party
Left , 'Lakeside Paisley
Print'

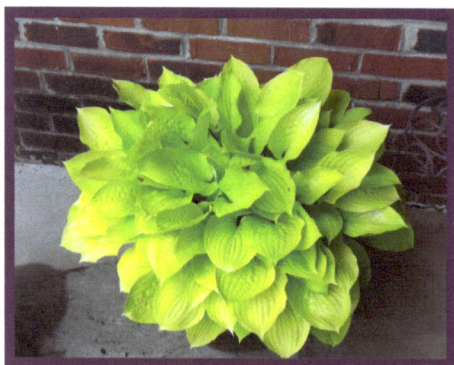

'Fire Island'

On the other side of the tiny back yard, Hosta 'Orange Marmalade' grows under a small tree, accompanied by yellow Asiatic lilies and Hakonechloa grass.

Hostas usually turn yellow in the fall and provide bright color when located in an area where they are accompanied by lovely fall foliage. The pots on this bank were located under a red maple and created a pretty fall picture among the fallen red leaves. Hostas truly provide all-summer beauty in your garden.

'Dinner Mint'

Hosta 'Mango Salsa'

When winter winds are blowing
it's hard to look ahead.
But better days will come again.
Think Spring! Think flowerbeds!

Wood poppies bloom bright yellow,
they'll dispel the gloom.
Before you even know it,
azaleas, too, will bloom.

And then one day you'll notice
lovely patterns have appeared.
The hosta leaves have now unfurled
unique colorations for this year.

THE LITTLE ONES

Do you have a small yard? Do you think hostas are pretty? Why not grow them in pots or troughs on your deck or patio? Lots of little ones are available, and as long as they are not in too much sun and are watered regularly, they are perfectly happy in containers.

When I first became aware of the little ones, there were only a few available. But in the last 20 years, many named little ones (mini hostas) have been introduced. And they are so popular that they have their own category in the annual popularity survey by the American Hosta Society.

Many of the little ones are descended from the species *Hosta venusta*, a tiny green hosta. The *Hosta Journal*, the magazine of the American Hosta Society, had an article about this species in a recent issue, and it was noted that *venusta* is from the Latin word *venustus*, meaning beautiful and graceful. Several of the cultivars mentioned in that article are ones I have grown: 'Tiny Tears,' 'Masquerade,' and 'Imp.' Two little ones developed by Mary Chastain of Ooltewah, Tennessee have been favorites of mine: 'Lakeside Neat Petite' and 'Lakeside Miss Muffet.'

The Hosta of the Year 2008, 'Blue Mouse Ears,' was the first little hosta to be chosen for that honor. It is a unique little hosta with heavily textured, rounded blue leaves, and it usually stays No. 1 on the Popularity Poll for mini hostas. It's a good grower, and it blooms with a mass of lavender blossoms. (The one shown here has been in its pot for at least ten years). It came on the hosta scene with a bang, and its descendants, the "mice," are a collector's dream. There are now many of them—green, blue, and yellow ones, and many have variegated leaves. Even ruffles.

'Blue Mouse Ears'

'Church Mouse'

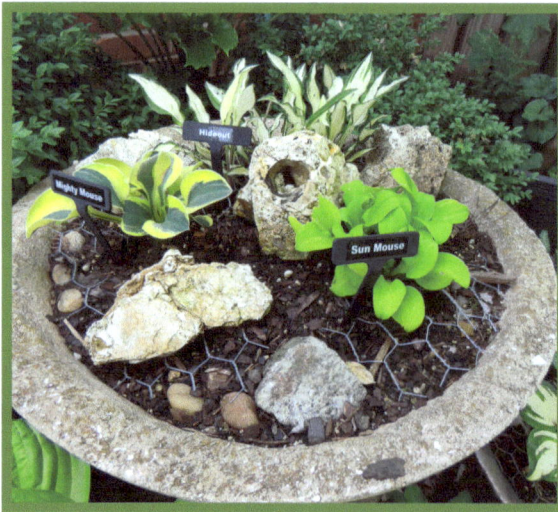

'Mighty Mouse', 'Hideout', 'Sun Mouse'

The first little hostas I bought were Hostas 'Ginko Craig' and 'Chartreuse Wiggles,' which is still one of my favorites. I planted them among my other hostas and thought they looked pretty there. But there were two problems: 1) The slugs and snails had too easy access to them on the ground. 2) The other, larger plants quickly overwhelmed them. So, it is best to dedicate a special place in your garden for the little ones (maybe a raised bed) or grow them in pots. This picture shows a blue bowl containing 'Chartreuse Wiggles' and 'Giantland Mouse Cheese.'

Another popular descendent of 'Blue Mouse Ears' is 'Mini Skirt.' When I bought this one, I enjoyed telling people, "Oh, I just bought a mini skirt." Then I'd watch them look astonished because they were pretty sure I wouldn't wear a mini skirt.

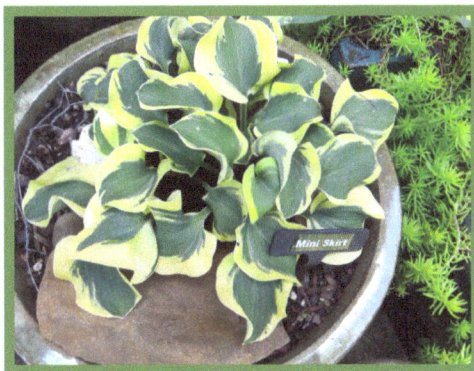

Two little hostas that just barely missed being classified as minis but are nevertheless very small are 'Fruit Loop' and 'Lakeside Dimpled Darling.' These are two of my favorite hostas because they have absolutely marvelous foliage.

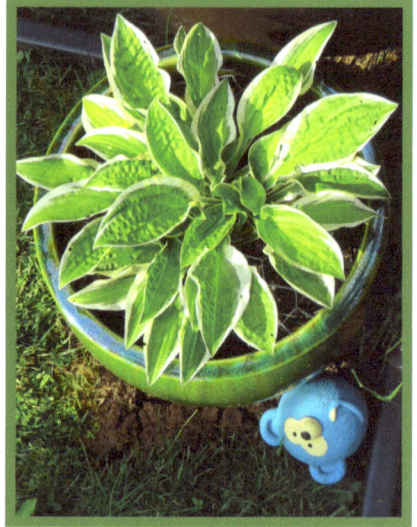

I bought three new ones in spring, 2021. In the *North American Rock Garden Society Quarterly* in the fall 2020 issue, there was an article about preparing a crevice container using flat rocks. I decided to try this for myself, so this is the result. The little variegated one is Hosta 'Country Mouse,' the green one 'Green Thumb,' and the yellow one is 'Wonderful.' All three bloom beautifully and appear to be happy. ('Country Mouse' is not descended from 'Blue Mouse Ears,' but I think 'Green Thumb' is.)

The determination of what constitutes a mini hosta is that its leaves cannot be larger than those of 'Blue Mouse Ears' (or leaf blade area must be less than 6 square inches). The very smallest hosta I have grown is this one: H. 'Itsy Bitsy Spider.' The largest of the tiny leaf blades in my container measures 3/8" x 2." Isn't it cute?

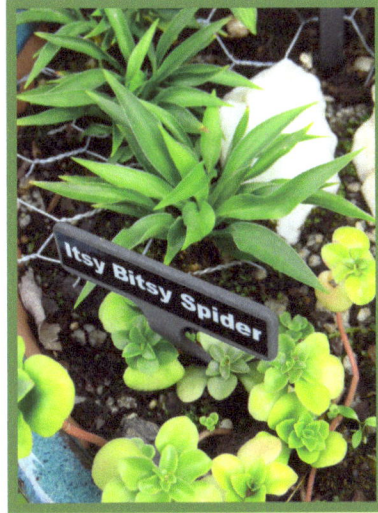

It is so much fun to compose a bowl of little hostas and companions. Pretty rocks, miniature conifers, little figures, and other miniature plants are candidates. "Fairy Gardens" are very popular, and many of the garden centers are stocking adorable things with which to compose a tiny garden scene. A 16-inch pot can contain three plants: hostas or companion plants. Be careful that other plants you choose to accompany your hostas are also tiny. A very small fern (*Athyrium felix-femina* 'Minutissima') can sometimes be found. There are also tiny conifers that make great companions.

Blue Mouse Ears was the original
Of my collection of little mice.
My little tiny hostas
Have been ever so nice!

Mighty Mouse was the second one.
Snow Mouse the next one I knew.
Sun Mouse's gold shines brightly;
Green Thumb blooms a purple hue.

Church Mouse has some ruffles,
Mini Skirt is ruffled, too.
Every single mouse is lovely.
I love them! That's really true!

HOSTA BLOSSOMS

Apparently, when hostas produce their buds, some on long stems, some people cut them off and think this improves the appearance of the foliage on their plants. Not me. I love hosta blossoms and consider hostas to be blooming plants like all the other perennials that bloom in my yard.

The height of the flowers varies on different varieties. Many lift their flowers high over the crown—a lot of the big hostas hold their flowers on long stems. This type is shown in the above picture. However, a lot of the mini hostas bear their flowers closer to the foliage. I tend to appreciate this type of flowering. The mini hosta, 'Blue Mouse Ears' has flowers that bloom close to its leaves, and most of its descendants bloom this way, too. And some recently developed hostas have petioles (stems) that are purple.

Another difference is color. A lot of hostas have white blossoms, especially those that are descended from *H. plantaginea*, the species from southern China that blooms in late summer with tall, white, fragrant blossoms. Here are a few of the different types.

'Guacamole'

'Biscuits & Honey'

'Green Thumb'

'Snow Mouse'

Here are some visitors. There are many sizes of bees all the way down to the tiny "sweat bees." All of them adore hosta flowers. It's so much fun to watch a bee disappear into a hosta blossom. I've even seen hummingbirds come to hosta flowers. I don't know why the Blue Dasher dragonfly or the wasp stopped by—they are not supposed to drink nectar.

'Lakeside Paisley Print'

'Lemon Snap'

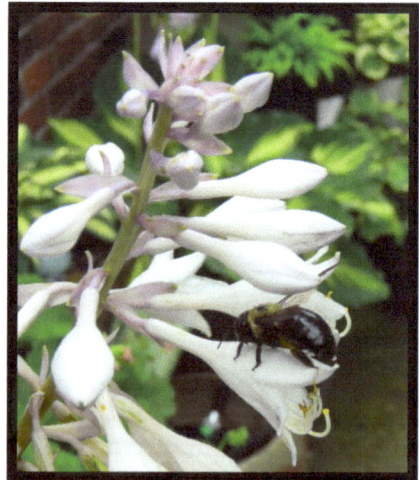

'Biscuits & Honey'

These are some of my all-time favorites.

'Blue Mouse Ears' and 'Lakeside Ninita'

'Lakeside Paisley Print (below)

Above, 'Lakeside Neat Petite'

Many hostas will produce a lot of seeds, especially the large varieties. They are easy to grow, but most will not result in a plant that matches the mother plant. In particular, seeds from a variegated plant will produce many seedlings that will revert to a solid color. Years ago, the ETHS visited the Ooltewah, Tennessee display garden of Mary Chastain, a hybridizer who developed many hostas with the first name 'Lakeside.' Many of her hybrids have been favorites of mine. She told us that of a thousand seedlings, she might have one that she would decide to keep.

Here are seed pods on 'Guacamole.' Of course, the pods on smaller hostas are also smaller, but almost all hostas will produce some seed pods.

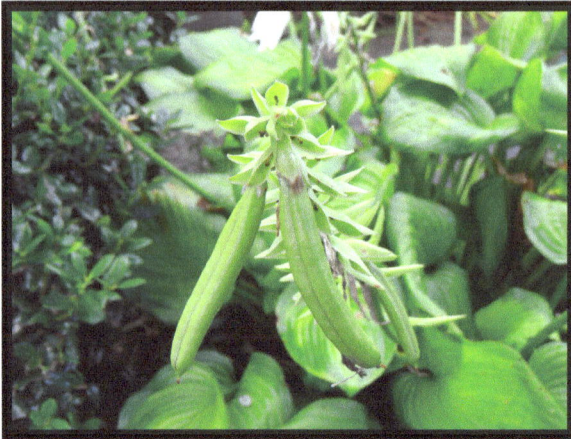

Today, a lot of the new hostas are developed through tissue culture mutation. Hostas are now prepared for sale by a laboratory procedure called "tissue culture" whereby tiny pieces of a particular variety are developed into clones of the original. Sometimes a mutation will appear that is different, and many new varieties are showing up now because of this procedure.

Another way new hostas are developed is that a plant with different characteristics might develop in a hosta clump. They are called "sports."

This is my pot containing 'Lakeside Dimpled Darling'. A sport with lighter color and less dimpling showed up in 2021. Can you see it in this picture? I have moved it to another pot to see how it behaves. If I think it deserves attention, I might register it as a new named variety. (Maybe "Green Darling"???)

'Lakeside Dimpled Darling'

Close-up

I think my most beautiful variety since I moved into my condo is 'Orange Marmalade.' This one was developed by Bob Solberg, the North Carolina hosta guru. Many of my hostas were purchased from him.

The other major source of my hostas is my good friend, Brian White of White's Nursery. I think he has been the single major reason the East Tennessee Hosta Society has remained a viable club for so long!

And the variety that blooms latest is 'Twist Tie' (below). That picture was made in mid-September. Hostas bloom in my garden all summer long, and I sit in my swing and watch the bees check them out.

Consider the wrens
My noisy good friends
Searching for bugs in the garden.

And see how the bees
Examine the trees
And flowers—for bright yellow pollen.

Watch butterflies flit
Then sip a bit
Of nectar in every bright blossom.

And I just observe
As they hover and swerve—
A panoply of nature happening!

COMPANION PLANTS

Hostas are marvelous! But with an equally beautiful companion they can be displayed even more beautifully. Over the many years that I have collected lovely hostas, they have been accompanied by many plants that I would recommend, and here are some of them.

The picture above included three of my favorite flowers. Hosta 'Liberty' is accompanied by marvelous Martagon lily, var. 'Album,' with its lovely cream-white blossoms. Beside them is a Larkspur plant that will add its blue blossoms after the lily is finished blooming. And on both sides are Impatiens, the quintessential summer annuals.

Next is another lily, a pink Asiatic, accompanied by Hosta 'Dark Star'. The lily was growing in the ground, but the hosta lived in a pot in front of the lily. And then there was my first, very young, Hosta 'Orange Marmalade' with a bright pink annual begonia blooming nearby. The bunny was one of my favorite non-blooming companions. Unfortunately, it was broken years ago when a limb fell from the overhead oak tree.

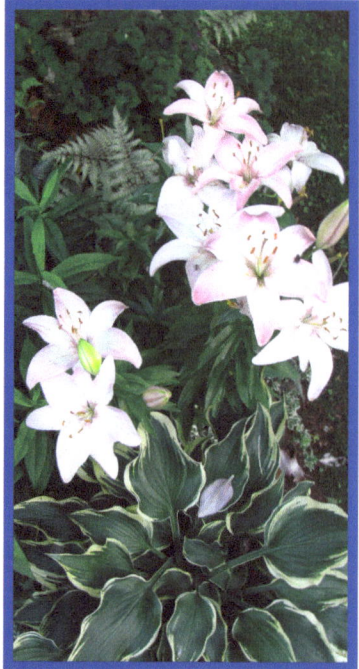

Right, 'Dark Star'

Below, 'Lakeside Orange Marmalade'

Elin Johnson

Hosta 'El Nino' is one of my favorites, shown here with a lovely clump of Japanese painted fern.

This bank may have been the most beautiful garden display I ever created. The picture was made in spring when the hostas were still small. But the ones in front of the azaleas were large ones, and later in the year they would take over as the main attraction.

This picture was made in front of the azaleas featuring the hostas, ferns and the foliage of a Pieris bush. This was the way the garden looked later in the summer.

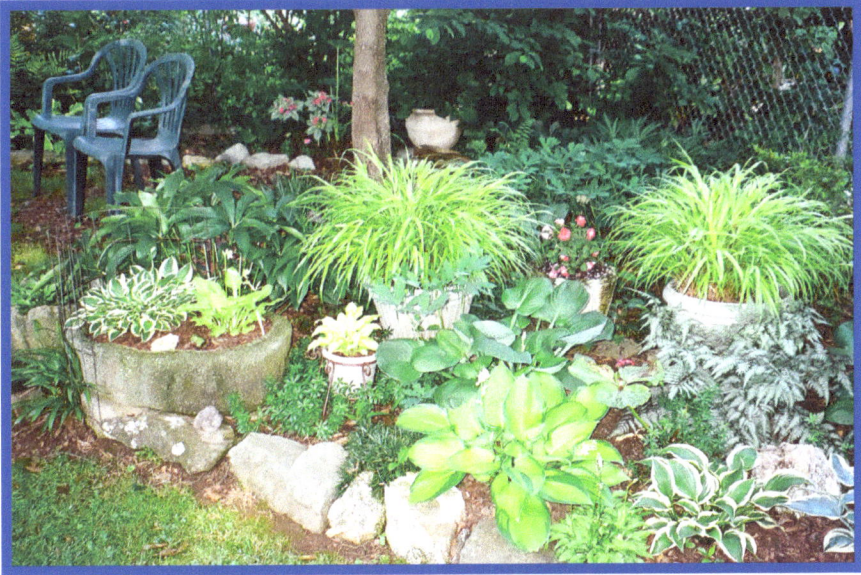

This was a view of the bed under a dogwood. The tree was given to me by a friend who had a cabin in the mountains. Containers of Hakonechloa grass were noticeable companions in this bed. I liked this beautiful grass so much that it has been included in all my later gardens including my current one. Also included were ferns and a clump of white Lenten Rose. Another constant you can see in this picture is the edging of rocks. This habit started with my grandmother, and I still expect my beds to have their rock edging.

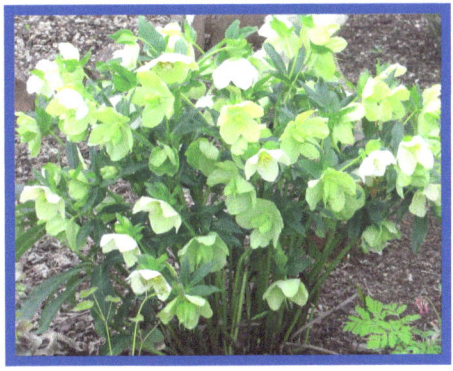

All of the pictures so far in this chapter were made in my first garden on Chestnut Street in Sweetwater. But then I moved to the house on Fairlane Drive. This was a flat, sunny yard where habitat for hostas was limited. But I spent half a year moving my favorite things to the new place. There were two oak trees behind the house, and that was where I started.

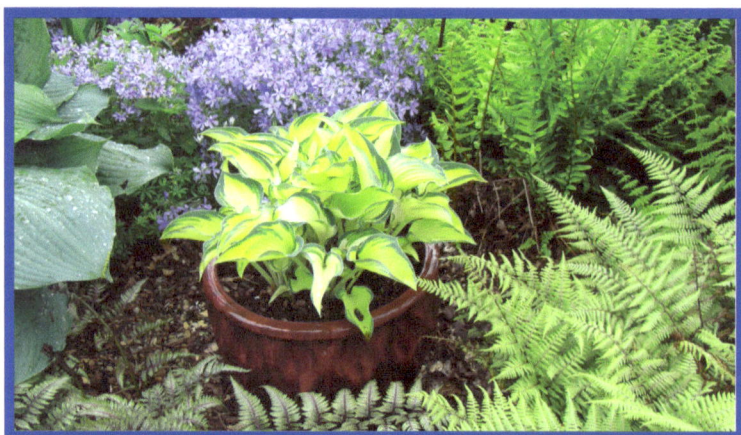

Ferns have been part of all my gardens. This hosta, 'What's That?' was surrounded by ferns: Top right was our native Christmas fern; below it to the right, Ghost fern; and along the bottom you can just see a Japanese painted fern. Blue wood phlox (*Phlox divaricata*) is another beauty that has accompanied many of my hostas in the spring.

In the picture below you can see the blue phlox with an emerging clump of Hosta 'First Frost,' as well as a clump of cinnamon fern. The other picture shows one of my Japanese painted ferns with its companion, a purple heuchera. Heucheras (coral bells) in many colors are another companion plant that have been present in most of my gardens.

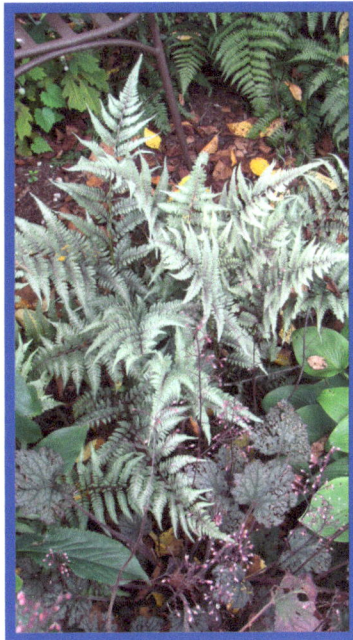

This bed at the end of the deck at my house on Fairlane Drive had many good companions. It changed from year to year. The picture below was made in the spring, and you can see ferns, columbines and blue phlox in bloom. There is also a clump of epimedium in the front right, and to the left are small celandine poppies, These two had finished blooming when the picture was made.

Columbines

Celandine poppies

Another picture of this bed, made in mid-summer, also features the ferns, and a Japanese maple with dark red foliage is present. That year, more of the hostas were present in their containers. Also present was a pot of Hakonechloa grass.

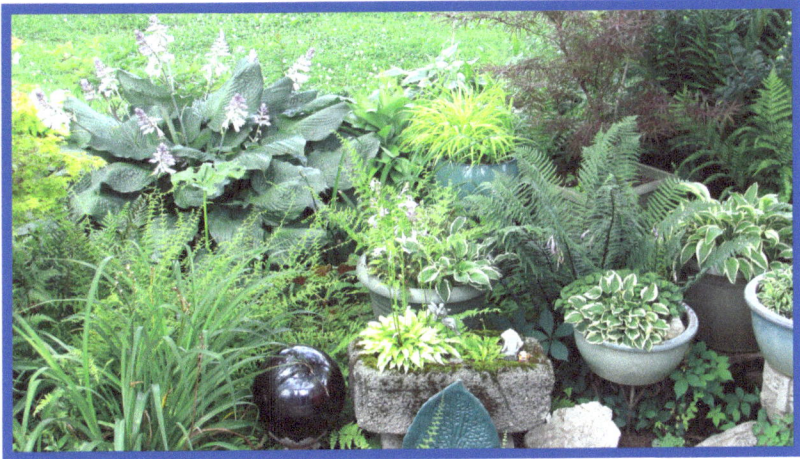

In the left-hand corner, you can see a clump of daylily. This was one of my all-time favorite plants, and you can see it in bloom in the picture below. (It still blooms at my condo.) At the corner of this bed a large clump of fountain grass decorated the path out into the back yard.

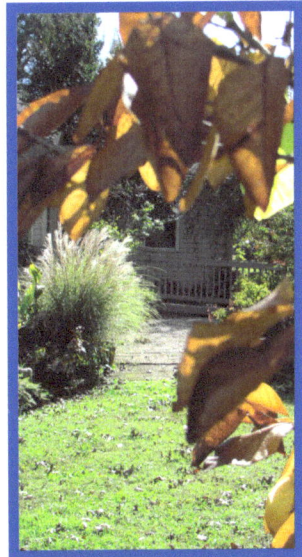

One of the oak trees died, and it was the one that had shaded the bed behind the deck all afternoon. That completely changed the character of this area, because the hostas were subjected to afternoon sun that was way too strong. So I placed some benches at the back of the garage and moved many of the containerized hostas out of the sun and into a sheltered place. Hosta 'First Frost' was the centerpiece, and a pot of Coleus provided color.

And then there was the "cherry bed." There was a large Japanese cherry tree that provided shade for a hosta garden, and lovely companions were planted there, too. This is the view you would see when you drove into the driveway, featuring Hosta 'Dandy Lion' and its neighbor, an oak leaf hydrangea.

This area was beautiful all summer. In the front was an early blooming Lenten Rose, and in late summer the hydrangea had beautiful color accompanied by pink hardy begonias. Then in the fall the hydrangea's leaves turned a lovely purple.

There were hostas all around the tree. Here on one side, Hosta 'June' lived, accompanied by 'Lakeside Prophecy Fulfilled' in its pot. There was a small daylily, a Japanese maple, a little gold heuchera, and a clump of tall sedum that provided a splash of pink in the late summer.

On the back side of the tree one of the *H. ventricosa* hybrids lived, and its blossoms created a lovely purple display in late summer. Pink American bleeding hearts (*Dicentra eximia*) planted next to it eventually spread its seedlings all around the hosta. Many of the seedlings had white blossoms. This area attracted hummingbirds all summer.

A pot of 'Praying Hands' was located on the west side of the tree, accompanied by hardy begonias behind and columbines in front.

Dicentra eximia

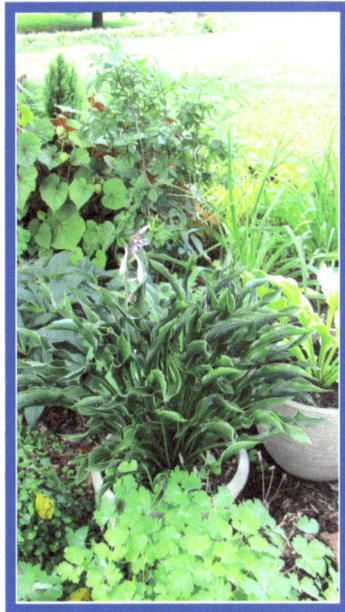

'Praying Hands'

Of course, bulbs bloomed around my hostas in early spring. Here you see white 'Ice Follies' daffodils and Lenten Roses blooming in a hosta bed.

See the hostas in their respective containers with their tiny cones pushing through. The pink flowers are *Corydalis solida*.

Early in the morning after a rain
New treasures now appear—
Small cones of green and purple
Bring promise for the year.

Soon they'll unfurl fresh new leaves
Variegated, green and blue.
Hostas—reawakening!
When spring rain gives the cue.

FROM MANY TO A FEW

I'm 85 years old as I write this. And I've been a gardener all of my long life. I've grown just about every flower you can think of at one time or another. Even had a vegetable garden for a number of years and canned tomatoes, green beans and pickles. But over the years the vegetables were replaced with perennials, and I've had two major flower gardens. Every time I moved, each new garden contained more hostas than the last, and their number finally topped one hundred.

But in 2018 I had to realize that I was no longer able to maintain a large garden, so I bought a condo in Knoxville to be close to my sister. I looked for a long time, and finally found a place where I could have a small back yard with room for a few flowers. This was paramount, not only for me but for my little dog, Sparky, to have a place to be outside.

But then came the hard part. What could I not bear to be without? I had to have daylilies. I had many varieties in the old garden, but I brought six to the new garden including one that I had kept from my grandmother's garden. She was my gardening mentor, and it is comforting to still have things I remember from her garden. It still blooms in the front yard of my condo next to Hosta 'Guacamole.'

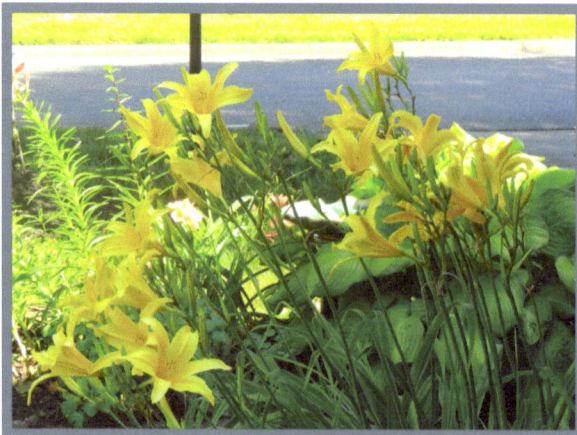

But the most important plants, of course, were my hostas. Fortunately, many were in pots, so they were not hard to move. I wound up keeping about thirty, and most were small to mini. I spend time sitting in my swing, looking across at my beautiful hostas. Here, Hosta 'Lakeside Paisley Print' is in bloom, accompanied by 'Bachelor Party' on top and 'Whee' to the side.

'Biscuits & Honey'

'Whee', 'Fruit Loop'
above

Hosta 'Dinner Mint' is one of my favorites, and from my swing I can watch it develop all summer in front of the table. It blooms profusely in late summer.

On down toward the corner, Hosta 'Lemon Snap' lends its beautiful yellow color between containers of mini hostas. It, too, has lovely blooms.

In the front yard, Hosta 'Guacamole' welcomes you, accompanied by Hostas 'Candy Dish,' 'What's That,' and 'Fire Island' in their respective pots. The window behind the daylilies is mine, but from there over is my neighbor's condo. Her rose bush is beautiful when it's in bloom.

Hostas have provided me with a great deal of pleasure for many years. They may not be as numerous now, but those that remain continue to entertain me throughout the summer. I look forward to their emergence in the spring, the unfurling of their beautiful leaves, watching the different varieties display their blossoms from early to late summer, and even the gold color of their fall foliage. I am a true hosta lover! Come and visit, and I'll show you my lovely companions!

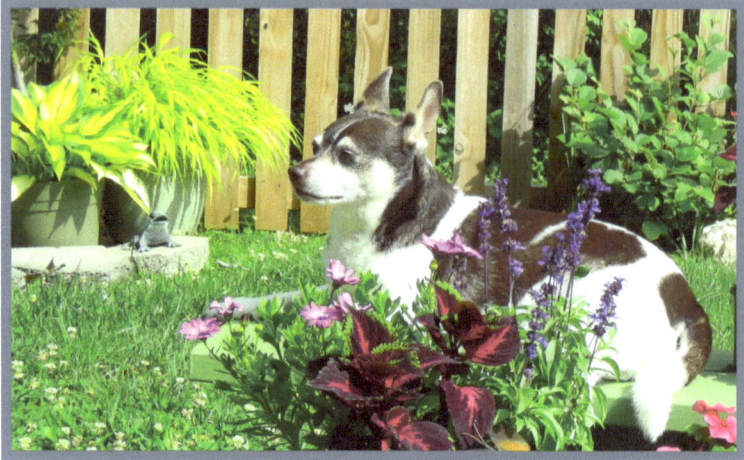

I used to look across the yard—
I took a longer view.
But now I look much closer
At what bees and butterflies do.

Now I sit in the swing and study
All the plants and Sparky, too.
When you're sitting still you notice
Just how the hostas grew.

I can still admire my favorites.
Pretty leaves are within my view.
I can even add new beauties
To my collection, too.

Elin Johnson

Elin Endsley Johnson, a native Tennessean, worked at a large paper mill for 33 years. She began gardening in earnest after her retirement, and during the next 20 years developed two gardens. One was a small lot on a steep hillside, divided into "garden rooms". It was mostly shady with mature trees and shrubs. Then she moved to a larger property with flat and sunny land. After retirement she has been a dedicated volunteer at the University of Tennessee Gardens, and became a Blount County, TN Master Gardener. She was one of the original members of the East Tennessee Hosta Society, which was formed in 1998. She now lives in a condo with a small garden in Knoxville, Tennessee where she is still able to enjoy many of her favorites—her lovely hostas.

Hostas: Memories of a Hosta Lover is her second book. Her first book, published in 2019, is Contemplation: A Year in the Garden. Elin has also written for several magazines and journals, including

REFERENCES:

East Tennessee Hosta Society **www.easttnhostasociety.com**

American Hosta Society **www.hostas.org**

For pictures and description of all registered hostas,
www.hostalibrary.org

RESOURCES:

www.brianwhitesnursery.com
Brian White is a charter member of the East Tennessee Hosta Society and my good friend. Many of my hostas have been purchased from his nursery in Maynardville, Tennessee.

www.hostahosta.com
Bob Solberg, of Green Hill Hostas in Franklinton, North Carolina is a major supplier of hostas and hybridizer. he is well-known to hosta lovers all over the country.

www.ingramcontent.com/pod-product-compliance
Lightning Source LLC
Chambersburg PA
CBHW040937030426
42335CB00001B/21